Things Mentally Strong People do: Build Resilience, Embrace Change, and develop Self-esteem

Drew R. Riker

Table of contents

Chapter 1

Preview of mental strength

There are moments when we feel like we can manage everything life throws at us. And then there are days when even the tiniest setback seems overwhelming. What makes the difference?

It's not the situations we encounter. Many of us know what it's like to be disturbed by something that wouldn't typically affect us. We frequently may then turn around and shrug off huge disappointments as simply being part of life.

The difference isn't what's happening: it's our mental power. Our mental power allows us to avoid getting distracted by negative ideas. It helps us get back into the ups and downs of life day after day. And — much like physical strength — it's a type of mental muscle that we can build to increase our general well-being.

What is mental strength?
Mental strength doesn't imply that you never weep, moan, or show uncertainty. And it's not mutually exclusive to mental disease. In reality, because they've had to work so hard to create coping methods, many individuals with ADHD, depression, and other mental health disorders are tremendously psychologically strong people.

Instead of having one set understanding of what it means to be mentally healthy, mental strength looks at these questions: How do you react to unpleasant feelings or setbacks? Do you start thinking about answers, moan about your poor luck, or let them roll off your back?

What is mental strength?

Mental strength is the cognitive and emotional ability to reframe negative ideas and difficult situations. Being mentally strong, or mentally tough, helps us withstand both internal and external pressures that impair our self-confidence and well-being.

We may utilize the metaphor of physical health to explain mental power. Just as physical strength is a component of physical fitness, mental strength is an aspect of mental fitness.

Mental fitness is the whole collection of behaviors that help you to maintain and develop your mental health. Mental toughness helps you remain concentrated in important situations — for example, the athlete who has to drown out the crowd to score a winning goal. Even if mental toughness helps you succeed under duress, it's typically not sustainable. Even with

Olympic athletes, this type of severe strain may affect mental health.

On the other side, mental strength balances the extreme. We can work successfully and sustainably in the face of obstacles and stress — without losing our health, sense of self, and mental well-being. It's strongly tied to resilience. And in reality, Olympic silver medal winners tend to be more resilient than gold medal winners.

To recap, resilience, mental strength, and mental toughness are all components of mental fitness. Mental toughness helps you filter out distractions and negative self-talk. Resilience helps you recover from setbacks. Mental power allows us to endure, and mental fitness strengthens all of these disciplines.

To be mentally healthy, we must build up our mental strength! Mental strength is something that is built through time by those who choose to make personal growth a priority. Much like witnessing physical advantages from working out and eating properly, we must create good mental habits, like practicing appreciation, if we want to see mental health gains.

Likewise, to experience physical advantages we must also give up bad behaviors, such as consuming junk food, and for mental gains, give up unhealthy habits such as feeling sorry for ourselves.

We are all able to get intellectually stronger, the trick is to continue practicing and training your mental muscles – just as you would if you were attempting to acquire physical strength!

New call-to-action

What is an example of mental strength in practice?

You're thrilled about a presentation that you'll be making shortly to the executives of your firm. You're practicing your slides, and your buddy points out a problem in your plan. You're thrown off, and you've put weeks of hard effort into preparing for this. Do you have time to rethink your whole presentation?

All isn't lost knowing the possible dangers might help you create a more well-rounded presentation. BetterUp discovered that the one activity that made more of an impact than any other for building future-minded leaders was visualizing the worst-case scenario. But getting into that solution-focused attitude — instead of panicking — demands mental power.

Instead of tossing the entire presentation trash or calling out ill, you decide to add another slide with your friend's worries. You utilize it as a jumping-off point to open the dialogue for questions and comments. The leaders are pleased not just with your hard work, but your genuineness and vision. Your mental power helped you to push beyond your anxieties and locate the silver lining.

mental-strength-person-doing-squats-focus ed-on-the-beach
The necessity of being mentally strong
In many respects, mental strength — and future-mindedness — is the flip side of worry in action.

When you think about what anxiety is and why it occurs, those terrible feelings do serve a function. Anxiety is meant to warn us of possible hazards so we may develop solutions to overcome them. But it becomes maladaptive (unhelpful) when the sensations of dread immobilize us.

Mental power helps us fight immobility and battle back against the effects of dread and worry. When we gain mental strength, we're better equipped to reframe the worry and hear what it's trying to tell us. What consequences do we need to think through?

What's the worst-case scenario? And how can we prepare for it to optimize our chances of success?

Mental strength influences us in other significant ways, too. Here are 5 advantages of building mental strength:

1. Less stress

When you're psychologically strong, you're less stressed by the things that happen in life - huge or little. You regard difficulty as a chance to progress. Even when major things happen, you're able to reframe them and have faith that you'll get through them. After all, you've gone through big things before.

Managing your stress is one of the most effective methods to enhance your overall well-being. Decreased stress levels are connected with a lower risk of depression, anxiety, and various physical health issues.

2. Motivation

Poor mental strength saps our energy and drive. We feel that no matter what we attempt to accomplish, awful things happen and nothing ever works out.

On the other side, mentally powerful persons have a high internal locus of control. That suggests that people feel that they have control over their circumstances. That feeling of control pushes people to keep trying, improving, and seeking answers. Resilient folks don't give up easily.

Mental strength also gives the discipline and internal drive required to resist procrastinating. Psychologically tough people have an easier difficulty getting started and finishing activities.

3. Discretion

Part of being successful in life is understanding what to listen to — and what not to listen to. It's easy to be thrown off by both internal and external criticism. When you acquire mental toughness, it becomes much simpler to remain focused, even when others disagree with you or you feel terrified.

Discretion is also crucial to developing self-awareness, and in turn, emotional management abilities. As you learn to sit with your bad feelings, you'll acquire a higher tolerance for them. Over time, you'll learn which emotions are worth connecting with and which ones to simply let go of.

4. Courage

When we feel psychologically powerful, we're less terrified of failure. Even if we're scared about the possible consequence, it's simpler for us to change into problem-solving mode. Our self-belief is greater, so we feel more sure in our capacity to discover answers. More significantly, we feel comfortable that we can withstand the worst-case situation (if it does come to occur) (if it does come to pass).

5. Adaptability

Developing our capacity to explore for answers makes us more nimble and adaptive. We spend less time worrying about what's not going well and more time focused on how we might reach the intended objective. We're also open to the thought that there can be more than one road, answer, or conclusion that shows success. We don't become tied to having everything go precisely our way, since we're not terrified of change.

Chapter 2

They don't feel sorry for themselves

Whether an economic slump has taken a toll on your money account, or you're suffering from a chronic health problem that interferes with your normal life, hardship is unavoidable. But the manner you manage life's unavoidable obstacles is up to you.

You may either make the most of a bad circumstance or you can dig in your heels and wallow in some real self-pity. Choosing to feel sorry for oneself, though, has some major repercussions.

It will rob you of the mental power you need to be your best. And it might keep you caught in an unhealthy cycle of despair.

Sadness is a natural, healthy emotion. Feeling a little sorrowful might help you honor something that you've lost. And allowing oneself to feel miserable for a time is crucial to mending an emotional wound.

Self-pity is different, however. It goes beyond healthy melancholy. When you feel sorry for yourself, you'll magnify your misfortune and experience a sensation of despair and powerlessness.

You can start believing that your life will never be good again. And you could assume that no one could help make you feel better. This type of thinking is self-destructive.

Self-pity creates an unhealthy loop. You'll start to feel any effort you make into altering your life will be meaningless. Consequently, you won't take any action and you'll be locked in a gloomy spot.

Whether you want to avoid self-pity, or you've already begun feeling sorry for yourself and want to stop, these two psychological methods will put an end to the pity party:

When you find yourself in the thick of a pity party, you'll be inclined to spend your energy being trapped there. Rather than address your issues, you'll waste time saying prospective solutions simply won't work.

You'll also likely find yourself moaning about the injustice of your circumstances in an attempt to convince other people to join your pity party. And although your criticisms may help you win some brief sympathy, your efforts will ultimately wreak havoc on your social life.

Commiserating with those around you isn't exactly a bonding activity. After all, no one ever says, "What I truly enjoy about her is that she feels sorry for herself." And as you reject others, you'll be more prone to plunge further into self-pity.

So it's important to adjust your conduct. Do actions that make it tougher to indulge your apocalyptic ideas.

This may require getting up off the sofa and getting active. Physical exercise may do wonders for your mental and emotional wellbeing. So go for a stroll, do a jog, or start cleaning the home. Moving your body may affect your perspective.

You may also do something good for others. Volunteer for a charity, aid a friend, or just locate someone in need. Kind deeds remind you how much you can offer to others and keeps you from being focused on what you believe other people should be doing for you.

While self-pity encourages you to believe "I deserve better," appreciation is about thinking, "I have more than I deserve." And altering the way you think may fend against self-pity while also enhancing your life in many other ways.

Studies suggest appreciation delivers several advantages ranging from better sleep and increased health to stronger mental power and better stress resistance.

There are various methods to cultivate appreciation. You may write in a thankfulness diary every evening. Or, you may make it a practice to think of three things you're thankful for every time you're tempted to whine about how horrible your life is.

The goal is to develop a thankfulness method that works for you. When you begin to notice what you have to be grateful for, you'll no longer be inclined to hold a pity party.

Giving up self-pity will make you psychologically stronger. And the stronger you grow, the simpler it is to keep self-pity away.

Refusing to feel sorry for yourself assures that you won't squander important time and precious energy wishing things were different. Instead, you'll be ready to take the constructive action you need to address difficulties, manage your pain, and build a healthy mindset.
Whether you've failed to clinch a significant transaction, or you're burdened by an impending deadline, hosting a pity party won't help. Feeling sorry for oneself may become downright self-destructive. It makes overcoming hardship tough – if not impossible – and it keeps you entrenched.

Mentally strong individuals refuse to allow self-pity to destroy their accomplishments. Instead, they utilize life's unavoidable trials as an opportunity to grow stronger and become better. Here's how psychologically strong individuals escape the self-pity trap:

1. They Face Their Feelings

Mentally strong individuals allow themselves to face emotions like loss, disappointment, and loneliness head-on. They don't divert themselves from unpleasant feelings by asking if their issues are fair, or by telling themselves they've suffered more than others around them. They realize the best way to cope with pain is to simply go through it.

2. They Recognize Warning Signs of the Downward Spiral

When you concentrate on everything that is going wrong in your life, your thoughts become exaggeratedly negative. And those negative ideas will adversely affect your conduct if you linger on them. The combination of negative thoughts and inaction fosters additional sentiments of self-pity. Mentally strong individuals realize when they're in danger of being entangled in this downward cycle and they take action to protect themselves from living a wretched existence.

3. They Question Their Perceptions

Our emotional state determines how we view reality. When you're feeling sorry for yourself, you're apt to concentrate on the negative things going on in your life, while neglecting the positive. Mentally powerful individuals wonder if their ideas reflect reality.

They ask themselves things such as, "Is my luck always bad?" or "Is my whole existence ruined?" Asking oneself these sorts of questions assists people to understand when their viewpoint isn't realistic. This permits individuals to build a more realistic perspective of their circumstances.

4. They Turn their Negative Thoughts into Behavioral Experiments

Mentally powerful individuals don't let their negative thoughts evolve into self-fulfilling prophecies. Instead, when they find themselves thinking things like, "I could never put on a presentation as fantastic as this one," they answer by stating, "Challenge accepted!" They do behavioral tests to show their negative thinking erroneous.

5. They Reserve their Resources for Productive Activities

Every minute you waste throwing your pity party is 60 seconds you postpone working on a solution. Mentally strong individuals refuse to squander their valuable time and energy concentrating on their sorrow. Instead, they dedicate their restricted resources to useful pursuits that might better their circumstances.

6. They Practice Gratitude

It's hard to feel self-pity and appreciation at the same moment. While self-pity is about thinking, "I deserve better," thankfulness is about thinking, "I have more than I need." Mentally strong individuals understand everything that they have to be thankful for in life – even down to the pure air to breathe and clean water to drink.

7. They Help Other People

It's hard to feel sorry for yourself when you're assisting less fortunate people. Problems like demanding customers or diminishing sales don't seem so awful when you're reminded that there are individuals who need food and shelter. Rather than obsess about their difficulties, psychologically healthy individuals attempt to enhance the lives of others.

8. They Refuse to Complain

Venting to other people about the extent of your issues fosters sentiments of self-pity. Mentally strong individuals don't attempt to elicit sympathy from others by moaning about their bad situations. Instead, they either take action to make things better, or they accept the realities that they can't alter.

9. They Maintain an Optimistic Outlook

Some of life's difficulties can't be avoided nor solved. The death of loved ones, natural calamities, and certain health ailments are challenges that most individuals will experience at one point or another. Mentally strong individuals have a positive view of their capacity to manage whatever life throws their way.

Build Mental Strength

Developing mental strength is analogous to growing physical strength. If you wanted to become physically powerful you'd need excellent habits - like lifting weights. But you'd also need to get rid of undesirable habits, like eating too many sweets. Developing mental strength involves excellent habits – yet it also demands you to give up detrimental habits, like self-pity.

Everyone can build mental strength. By acquiring a greater capacity to govern your thoughts, manage your emotions and act effectively despite your surroundings, you'll grow stronger and become better.

Chapter 3

They don't shy away from change. Change is constant, be ready for it

“nothing changes if nothing changes.” That may be a hard pill to swallow, particularly if you are lacking the drive to change, or have a fear of change. If you’re seeking to grow more mentally strong, accepting change is the way to go. So, what’s holding you back? Dig deep and take time to think about it.

You may have an underlying dread in your thoughts that you’ve embedded in your brain unconsciously. It’s normal for folks who dread change to have a wish to avoid negative sensations like loss, anxiety, despair, etc... This is a terrible fact that requires addressing if you are sincerely willing to better yourself. You can do it! We’re here to assist. Listen to episode 114 to discover how to accomplish this (scroll up and select play) (scroll up and hit play).

John had arrived with the issue of being 88 pounds overweight at the age of 34. He had resolved that daily after work he would go to the gym. But that concept of exercising was constantly put to the following day due to his exhaustion after his day at work. He then came to know that he was diagnosed with diabetes, which made him recognize that he had to quit eating garbage. He began off by tossing all his junk food away but after two days he found that he was back to consuming crap. He knew that he had gone back to what he was doing previously.

He and his wife then began taking this procedure carefully by collaborating. They determined that he would go to the gym 4 days a week. Slowly he could sense a shift, although the sugar level in his blood remained high. Now, anytime he wanted a snack he would select a portion of healthy food. Slowly he changed and now has managed to lose weight and reduce the sugar level in his blood.

This is how John worked towards transforming himself, but he learned one thing that change did not come at once. It is a long process and it takes time... As soon as he began making progress, he found it easy to make further adjustments. Eventually, he was able to feel more driven to reduce weight and regulate his blood sugar.

It's not unusual to worry about the repercussions of change. Whether it comes from our own choices or circumstances beyond our control, change in our personal and professional lives may be daunting, but it's frequently vital to keep developing and changing.

Instead of dreading change, embrace it and regard it as a good factor in your life. Here are some of the most successful tactics to attempt.

1. Prepare For It

If you realize change is required for your progress, prepare for it! Start small by taking adjustments that are not too unpleasant, like drinking more water vs attending a HIIT class or reading every day before applying for college classes. Ease your way into change, making it more manageable when big changes come. Once you see all the positives from the adjustments, you'll be ready for more!

2. Determine The Value

This may seem straightforward, but to create change, we have to establish the worth of the change. We're human and being human implies we don't do things merely for the sake of doing them, we require purpose, meaning, or advantage out of our activities. We'll undertake huge changes that we're enthusiastic about, such as getting married, relocating, or going to college, but other changes need thinking before action.

3. Keep Your Skills Current

To progress, accepting change is not optional. To adapt effectively, a smart method is to be conscious of your position by periodically asking yourself questions such as what is your goal, purpose, and what barriers stand in your way—this will help you grasp change and assist you to gain skills. Keeping your skills updated is a smart method to add to your value and progress.

4. Think About The Possibilities

Change is a crucial stage in the development process, and accepting change is all about having the correct mentality. Being interested and devoting yourself to identifying the benefits and learning possibilities in a particular scene rather than the barriers and difficulties will help you to get the required perspective and orient yourself toward positive and purposeful action.

5. Always Run Toward Only What You Want

Change can be scary and let's face it: Change is a permanent state today. Want to achieve gracefully when change occurs? Try this: Match your greatest ideals and abilities to the desired transformation. If they show up in what you are aiming to accomplish, race hard toward that transformation. If they do not show up at all, then find another path to reach where you want to go. — John Hittler, Evoking Genius

6. Allow Change To Reveal Your Strengths

Change forces us to react to new knowledge, events, and settings. It examines our capacity to achieve while adapting in new and innovative ways and gauges our resilience and personal agency. Recognizing change as a revolutionary agent of exposure and leadership potential empowers us to dread it less and welcome it as a partner in constructing a more satisfying and genuine existence.

7. Redefine Change To Be Your 'Nirvana'

Redefining change as a chance to reach your desired result is a crucial mentality to embrace. Who wouldn't leap at the opportunity to make a good influence on their terms? By imagining your “nirvana” end outcome and working toward reaching it, you will more likely remain motivated to see the effects of the techniques you adopt since they are linked with your interests.

8. Don’t View Relapses As Failure

People anticipate developments will move upward. They anticipate blockages, but if they resort to previous methods of behavior, they assume it is over and stop totally. A person could have some or many modest lapses or relapses. The key to transformation is to realize that, rise, brush yourself down and come back to the desired habit. The secret to success is to not allow these failures to impair your self-confidence.

9. Be Consistent In Your Actions And Motivation

Irrelevant from the aim of the change, consistency in activities is important. Wanting to create change will necessarily demand consistent behaviors, which in turn is also one of the key reasons why desired outcomes can't be attained without it. It needs a process that leads to constant behaviors that are substantially impacted by consistent motivation.

10. Don't Just Embrace Change; Drive It

People have decried change and the velocity by which things change for millennia. With technology developments producing seismic upheavals in all parts of life and with information doubling happening on average every 13 months, there is no time to "work to embrace" change. Today, change creates either growth or decline. The future is being constructed today and change catalysts have the advantage.

11. Get An Accountability Partner

Scared by change? Others are too. And they want to help you and themselves change. Make them your accountability partner. Research demonstrates that the more you follow up with your accountability partner, the more improvement you will accomplish. I check in with my accountability buddy, Paul, every week. We let go of what didn't serve us well the past week, celebrate wins and give advice for the week ahead.

12. Create An Achievable Roadmap To Change

Everything occurs in measured time. We must design an attainable plan. The most effective technique to reach this objective is a timeframe and a plan. Every piece of time must be planned for. Once you have established your timeframe, you may prepare! Developing an action plan together with knowing how the change may be sustained builds successful habits. Predictability will provide serenity and tranquility.

13. Reduce The Ambiguity

Change is terrifying because it generates uncertainty. When we aren't sure what's on the other side, our brains move us to survival mode. When possible, seek answers or clarification on the shift, and when they aren't known, take time to contemplate all of the possibilities. When you can see a range of possibilities ahead, the uncertainty is eased and we may lean in to develop from the shift.

14. Make Change An Adventure

Our words and perceptions matter and affect our behavior and actions. Reframing the way we think about change is incredibly essential in whether we worry about it or we welcome it. Stop thinking about change as the big bad wolf—"scary," "uncertain" and "negative"—and start thinking about change as an adventure and a joyful experience where we will learn and develop and have fun in the process.

Chapter 4

Do not concentrate on things you can't control

When things don’t go our way, it’s so simple to become immersed in the erroneous idea. We float into areas and thoughts we have no authority over. We start obsessing over all the things that aren’t working in our favor, thinking about all the horrible things that may happen next. We muddle our judgment and lose awareness of our involvement in making our world.

Such may be the situation now.

We’re battling through challenging situations. I can promise you every one of us is experiencing good days and terrible days.

On the good days, we attempt to be cheerful and productive. On the terrible days, we sulk under the stress of forecasting what the future is going to be like. We picture it, and then we start experiencing it, which leaves us feeling powerless and afraid.

That's because ideas truly do produce your feelings.

Thought fires before emotion, then your brain connects. You repeat that URL enough, and it begins running automatically.

Thoughts fire before emotions—that's why when we think poorly, we experience unpleasant feelings.

But there's a way around this.

Whenever you notice yourself drifting from an optimistic viewpoint to a negative one, do your best to bring your focus back to the most essential component of all.

Ask yourself these three questions:

- What is bothering me?
- What is under my control?
- What matters most to me and what can I do about it?

When we concentrate on what we can manage, our ideas strengthen us and then produce pleasant feelings.

Happiness and freedom begin with a clear knowledge of one principle: Other things are under our control, and some things are not. The primary challenge in life is essentially this: to identify and divide items so that I can declare clearly to myself which are externals not under my control, and which have to do with the decisions I truly control.

This one idea is at the heart of how we approach life:

Do we throw our power away to elements we cannot control or do we maintain it and focus our energy on the possibilities we can genuinely influence?

When your mind plays tricks on you and slips you into a torrent of concern, deliberately strive to swim out of it.

All You Need to Know: Within our power are our views, attitudes, ambitions, hopes, objectives, and goals. We choose how we spend our time, what literature we read, how productive we are, what we eat, the number of hours we choose to sleep, and who we choose to spend time with.

Outside our control lies everything else: the family and body you were born into, how life's events occurred, the weather, the economy, other people...

Trying to control or modify what isn't within your power will just deplete your energy and leave you in anguish. What you can control is how you perceive a situation, how you react to it, and how you respond.

The fact is this: Even though you may not like the circumstance you are in, you can choose to accept it. Once you learn to accept what is, and then concentrate on what you can control, you win.

Chapter 5

You can not develop your mental strength if you are a people pleaser

People-pleasers are recognized for doing whatever it takes to make other people happy. While being nice and helpful is typically a good thing, going too far to satisfy others may leave you feeling emotionally tired, agitated, and nervous.

Signs You Might Be a People-Pleaser

There are a lot of features that people-pleasers seem to share. Here are some clues that you could be a people-pleaser:

- You have a tough time saying "no."
- You are obsessed with what other people may think.
- You feel bad when you do tell someone "no."

- You worry that turning someone down may make them believe you are cruel or selfish.
- You consent to things you don't like or do things you don't want to do.
- You battle with emotions of low-self esteem.
- You want others to like you and believe that doing things for them will gain their approval.
- You're constantly telling folks you're sorry.
- You assume the blame even when something isn't your fault.
- You never have any spare time since you are constantly doing things for other people.
- You overlook your own needs to accomplish something for others.
- You pretend to agree with others even while you feel otherwise.
- People-pleasers tend to be skilled at listening to what others are experiencing. They are also typically

sensitive, thoughtful, and kind. These great attributes may also come with a bad self-image, drive to take control, or inclination to overachieve.

Effects of Being a People-Pleaser

pleasing people isn't always a negative thing. Being a concerned and caring person is a crucial aspect of sustaining strong connections with loved ones. It becomes a concern, though, if you are attempting to acquire acceptance to shore up poor self-esteem or if you are chasing the pleasure of others at the price of your emotional well-being.

If you are investing all of your time in helping others to make them happy and obtain their approval, you can face some of the following repercussions.

Anger and Frustration

While you could truly love helping, you are also certain to suffer aggravation when you are doing things grudgingly or out of duty. These sentiments might lead to a loop of assisting someone, feeling upset at them for taking advantage, and then feeling guilty or sad for yourself.

Anxiety and Stress

Efforts to make other people happy might strain your own physical and mental resources too thin. Trying to handle it all might leave you tormented with worry and anxiety, which can have harmful repercussions on your health.

Helping other people may truly offer a lot of mental health advantages.

But not allowing time for oneself means you can end up facing the negative health implications of extreme stress.Devoting all of your energy and mental resources to making sure that others are pleased implies you are less likely to have the determination and willpower to handle your objectives.

If you are utilizing your mental energies to make sure that other people have what they want or need, it can indicate that you simply have little left to dedicate to your own needs.

Lack of Authenticity

People-pleasers will frequently disguise their wants and preferences to appease other people. This might make you seem as if you are not living your life authentically—it may even leave you feeling as if you don't know yourself at all.

Tips to Stop People-Pleasing

Fortunately, there are certain measures that you can do to quit being a people-pleaser and learn how to balance your need to make others happy without losing your own.

Establish Boundaries

It's crucial to recognize your limitations, create clear boundaries, and then express those limits. Be upfront and detailed about what you're willing to take on. If it appears like someone is asking for too much, let them know that it's past the borders of what you are willing to do and that you won't be able to assist.

There are many other methods to build boundaries in your life to assist rein in your people-pleasing instincts. For example, you may only accept phone calls at particular hours to impose boundaries on when you are allowed to communicate.

You may also mention that you are only accessible for a set length of time. This may be useful since it assures that you have control over not just what you are willing to accomplish, but also when you are willing to do it.

Start Small

It may be hard to make a dramatic shift, therefore it is generally better to begin by expressing yourself in modest ways. Changing behavioral habits may be tough. In many circumstances, you not only have to retrain yourself—but you also have to concentrate on training the others around you to realize your boundaries.

Because of this, it might be good to start with simple measures that help you work your way to becoming less of a people-pleaser. Start with saying no to lesser requests, try expressing your opinion on something little, or ask for something that you need.

For example, try saying no to an SMS request. Then work your way up to telling folks "no" in person. Practice in various locations or circumstances such as while talking to salesmen, ordering at a restaurant, or even when interacting with co-workers.

Set Goals and Priorities

Consider where you want to spend your time. Who do you wish to help? What aims are you seeking to accomplish? Knowing your priorities might help you assess whether or not you have the time and energy to commit to anything.

If anything is sapping your energy or requiring too much of your time, take measures to solve the situation. As you practice creating those boundaries and saying no to things you don't want to do, you'll discover that you have more time to dedicate to the things that are important to you.

Try Positive Self-Talk

If you start to feel overwhelmed or inclined to succumb, build up your determination with positive self-talk. Remind yourself that you deserve to spend time for yourself. Your objectives are essential, and you shouldn't feel forced to throw up your time and energy on things that don’t please you.

Stall for Time

When someone asks for a favor, tell them you need some time to think about it. Saying "yes" immediately away might leave you feeling obliged and overcommitted while taking your time to answer a request can allow you the opportunity to consider it and determine whether it's something you truly want to undertake. Before you make a choice, ask yourself:

- How much time will this take?
- Is this something I truly want to do?
- How stressed am I going to be if I answer "yes?"

Research has also demonstrated that even a brief pause before making a choice boosts decision-making accuracy. By allowing yourself a minute, you'll be better able to correctly assess whether it is something you have the desire and time to take on.

Assess the Request

Another step in overcoming being a people-pleaser is to seek evidence that other people are trying to take advantage of your generosity. Are there folks who constantly appear to want something from you but are suddenly unavailable once you need them to return the favor? Or do some folks appear to be aware of your giving disposition and ask because they know that you won't say "no?"

If it seems like you're being influenced into doing things, take some time to examine the issue and determine how you want to handle the request. For repeat offenders or persons who keep arguing that you should assist, be strong and unambiguous.

Avoid Making Excuses

It's crucial to be straightforward when you say "no" and avoid blaming other responsibilities or making excuses for your inability to participate. Once you start explaining why you can't do something, you are providing people with a method to find holes in your reason. Or you may be giving them the chance to adjust their request to ensure that you can still do what they are asking.

Try adopting a definite tone when you deny something and avoid the impulse to offer needless information about your rationale. Remind yourself that "no" is a whole statement.

Remember that Relationships Require Give and Take

A good, healthy connection includes a certain degree of reciprocity. If one person is constantly giving and the other is always taking, it frequently signifies that one person is forgoing things that they need to guarantee that the other person gets what they desire.

Even though you like gratifying people, it is crucial to remember that they should also be taking measures to offer to you in return.

Help When You Want to Help

You don't need to give up being courteous and considerate. Those are desirable attributes that may lead to good, enduring partnerships. The trick is to assess your motives and goals. Don't undertake things solely because you fear rejection or desire the approval of others.

Keep doing excellent things, but on your terms. Kindness doesn't need recognition or rewards—it only demands a willingness to make things better for another person.

Chapter 6

They don't fear taking calculated risks

The phrases “risk” and “risk-taking” are commonly encountered in personal development and self-improvement materials. According to the Merriam-Webster dictionary, the risk is defined as “exposure to prospective loss or injury.” Like any life change, implementing adjustments to enhance health and boost wealth requires accepting risks. By changing, you are stepping out of your “comfort zone” and implementing new behaviors that are distinct and/or challenging. David Viscott, the author of over a dozen books, including Risking, suggests the following: “Keep reminding yourself that all successful individuals have taken a risk at some point and succeeded. Taking a step into the unknown is the beginning point of personal excellence.” An often referenced poem about risk finishes with the lines “To attempt at all...is to risk failure. But to risk, we must, for the greatest peril in life...is to risk nothing.” Virtually everything individuals accomplish in life entails some form of risk. Therefore, we are always considering the benefits and disadvantages of different acts. For example, while staking a dog outside for a walk to gain exercise, we risk slipping or being struck by a vehicle. Yet many individuals accept this risk to accomplish something that they like. People \soften determine that some things in life are “worth the risk” and undertake them anyhow. Personal risk appraisal may also be impacted by circumstances such as the weather, recent life experiences, and the presence of other people (e.g., a single guy riding a motorbike vs a married man with two children riding one). Not all dangers are created equally, though. Some hazards, such as extreme sports, smoking, and the use of illicit narcotics are harmful and/or unhealthy.

Others, such as taking $1,000 to a casino and counting on luck or dumping money into a poorly planned business endeavor, are imprudent. Then there are calculated risks, such as investing for the long term in a stock index fund or the steady weight reduction of 40 pounds over a year with a healthy diet and exercise. With calculated risks, you have a vision of where you want to go and a route to get there.

You boost the likelihood of success by studying a risk-taking activity (e.g., investing), planning and executing an action plan, maintaining focus on your objectives, and anticipating and overcoming difficulties along the road (e.g., stock market downturns) (e.g., stock market downturns).

Success comes from taking measured risks and either attaining your objectives or learning from disappointments. Risk-taking suggests that you have faith in your abilities to achieve but also embrace the chance of failure since errors are a feature of life. Even if you fail, though, risks may often be regarded as a "success" if you learn from the experience and strive to do better the next time.

A typical hurdle to risk-taking is fear, such as fear of failure, fear of rejection, fear of pain, fear of loss, fear of getting started, or fear of responses by other people. Some concerns are genuine while others are just False Evidence Appearing as Real (i.e. illogical beliefs) (i.e. irrational beliefs). Some \speople utilize the protective mechanism of fear to protect themselves from injury or loss. It isn't enjoyable to endure tough or unknown circumstances and many individuals would avoid them if at all feasible.

You May Have Heard Advice Such As "Go With Your Gut" Or "Listen To Your Heart" From Time To Time. People Usually Give Such Suggestions When You Can't Decide Whether Or Not You Should Take Certain

Decisions Or Risks. Such Advice Can Work For You But Only If You Are Taking Calculated Risks. But While Doing So, Don't Confuse Your Fear With Your Gut Feeling And Give Up Before Even Starting.

What Is Calculated Risk-Taking? How Do You Decide If You Are Taking Foolish Or Calculated Risks? Let's Find Out.

Foolish Vs. Calculated Risk-Taking
There's A Big Difference Between Taking Foolish And Calculated Risks.

In Short, A Foolish Risk Is That Which You Take Without Doing Any Research Or Assessing The Possible Negative Consequences. You Would Be Moving Forward Blindly, Which Means That You Can Succeed Or Fail, But If You Fail The Consequences Can Be Huge As You Don't Know What's Waiting For You.

Calculated Risk-Taking, On The Other Hand, Involves A Fair Amount Of Research. Like It's With Taking Any Risk, The Results May Not Always Be Positive, But At Least You Will Have A Fair Idea Of What's In Store With You And The Chances Of Succeeding Or Failing.

Tips For Taking Calculated Risks
Now That You Know The Meaning Of Calculated Risk, Let's Find Out How To Measure Risk.

1. Do Research

Do Your Due Diligence Before Making A Decision. Calculated Risk-Taking Means Understanding Every Little Detail You Can About The Risk. This Will Help You Discover Any Red Flags And Potential Issues Beforehand, And You Will Be Ready With The Answers Or At Least Have A Fair Understanding Of The Possible Setbacks.

2. Anticipate Mistakes.

Smart Risk-Taker Anticipates Potential Mistakes Before Moving Forward. Think About Every Possible Outcome, Both Positive As Well As Negative.

Calculated Risk Examples Can Be Found In Financial, Mental, And Emotional Situations. So Ask Yourself Questions Like: What If The Deal Fails And You Lose Money, How Would Your Business Cope Up? If A Partnership Breaks, What Will Be The Next Course Of Action? If The Team Is Facing Some Setbacks, How Will You Meet Project Deadlines? Such Questions Can Help You Assess The Negative Outcomes And You Can Accordingly Figure Out How To Deal With Them.

3. Set Milestones And Goals

The Purpose Of Taking A Risk Is To Achieve A Certain Goal. Step Out Of Your Comfort

Zone To Achieve Something. It Could Be Anything From Signing Up A New Deal To Expanding Your Business.

However, Whatever The Goal, Know That It Could Take Months Or Even Years To Achieve It. So, How Do You Keep Yourself Motivated From The Start To The End? That's Where Your Carefully Assessed Milestones Will Come In Handy. Deciding On The Checkpoints In Between Is As Important As Setting Up The Goals.

4. Learn To Say "No"

Whether It's In Your Career Or Personal Life, Everyone Faces Situations Where They Have To Step Back And Say "No". But Not All Of Us Have That Skill, Especially When It Comes To Taking Potential Risks Or Opportunities.

However, Tempting And Beneficial It May Look, Jumping At Every Opportunity Will Exhaust You In The Long Run. You Won't

Have Enough Time And Energy To Take On The Ones That Probably Have A High Possibility Of Succeeding.

Every Business-Related Decision You Make Comes With Its Risks. Successful Entrepreneurs Know How To Take Calculated Risks And Assess Positive And Negative Outcomes. Have You Mastered The Calculated Risk-Taking Skills Or Are You Still Working On It? Harappa's Making Decisions Course Will Help You Develop And Master Calculated Risk-Taking Skills Through Various Easy Models And Frameworks. Join The Course And Get Going.

Chapter 7

Forget the past and move on

We frequently struggle to repair the scars in our life. These are scars and animosity from the past that continue to haunt us. There might be myriads of causes for these hurts—you were left out in the previous promotion, someone you held dear betrayed you, you were not treated well when exiting the organization you strived to develop, a person you rccruitcd, and fostered conspired to unseat you from your post. Someone plagiarised your novel and made it into a movie and did not even give acknowledgment. You believed your employer did not pay you your due. You suffered a nasty divorce. Though all the occurrences may not be the same, what they do is leave a lasting bitterness (in varying degrees of severity and length) (in varying degrees of intensity and duration).

Would you wish to spend your lovely life obsessing over something that's over? Or learn from it and go forward?
Interestingly, a friend of mine was once urged to never forget the scars of the past as it would in helpful in exacting retribution! How myopic. Would you wish to spend your lovely life obsessing over something that's over? Or learn from it and go forward?

Here's why I believe we should eschew the bitterness of the past.

1. You have one life

You have one life. Every minute in this world is important. Every contact, every event is unique and always has a valuable lesson. It's a kaleidoscope of experiences containing the good, the terrible, the unusual, the average, the amazing, the insignificant, the poisonous, and so on.

To put things in perspective, generally, it's a fantastic adventure, even if there are unpleasant times. How dull it would be if we only had things happen one way. It's the downs that sometimes make the ups more sparkling and fulfilling.

I believe we need to be more like ducks... they gulp down a load of things but swallow just what they want to consume, discarding the rest. We encounter wonderful things and bitter things, but it's crucial to preserve just the ones that make us better.

2. Time cures everything if you utilize it properly

Time cures everything. However huge a wound, it does heal over some time. However, to make it happen you need to utilize time properly. As a University of Arizona research discovered, people are not born resilient. They require a variable length of time to recuperate after a bad encounter. So one needs to focus on establishing this mental power. After a bitter experience, you have to take activities to overcome it. You have to occupy your attention with tasks that divert you from brooding and motivate you to go forward. This might include visiting a therapist, taking up new interests, adjusting behavior, etc.

Time will enable you to heal if you utilize it correctly. Otherwise, there's no certainty.

3. We might forget prior occurrences if we tamper with our context

We may forget the harsh recollections of the past if we have a desire to do so. One extremely efficient approach to achieve this is to do is to control or modify the context, according to a new study. We prefer to recall things among settings and context. The context comprises elements such as sights, sounds, times of day, etc.

Do something so significant and rewarding that when you reflect on the bitterness, you will feel glad to it for starting you on a better road.
So if you alter the context, and do not think about these clues or the scaffolding that went into the construction of memory, you tend to not recall the event. For example, if a song reminds you of an ex, listen to the music in a new context/environment such as on a morning stroll or when coming from work.

4. Forgiving is heavenly

People speak about physical strength, mental power, intellectual strength, etc. But one thing which people don't speak about is "forgiveness as a strength." If individuals cultivate forgiveness as a life skill they would have a much better existence. Forgiveness is the skill of letting go of the resentment and anger of the past that someone may have caused you. It's a purposeful attempt to get rid of bad thoughts regarding a person or group of individuals without carrying any grudge against them. Whether it's Hinduism, Buddhism, Islam, Christianity, Judaism, or Jainism—all faiths ask people to forgive those who have injured them. Forgiveness has many advantages. It relieves stress, helps to strengthen relationships, promotes self-esteem, lowers blood pressure, and improves general psychological wellness.

5. Workplace relationships aren't worth fretting over

Many of the connections we have with individuals in our office are transactional.

They are built on power equations, what you offer to the table. Many of the connections that you form are built on giving and taking.

People will remain with you as long as it suits their interest; the day they feel that you are of no service to them they will discreetly dump you. Have you not noticed how people interact with us when we are in a position of power and when we are out of it? As a matter of truth, your whole connection with your organization is built on what you provide to the table. While pleasant things will be said about your prior accomplishments, your presence in the organization is predicated on your future relevance, and not what you have achieved in the past. This may seem crass but it's the truth. So the point is, why obsess over professional occurrences when they are intrinsically transactional?

6. Disappointment is a chance to reinvent oneself

The greatest method to get over the after-taste of a previous bitterness is to attempt to achieve something worthwhile and reinvent yourself. Do something so significant and rewarding that when you reflect on the bitterness, you will feel glad to it for starting you on a better road. Don't we remember what happened to Steve Jobs? He was expelled from the firm he had built. He then went on to create NeXT and ultimately purchased Pixar. He returned to Apple when NeXT was purchased by Apple. As he said in the now famous Stanford graduating speech: "I didn't realize it then, but it turned out that being fired from Apple was the finest thing that could have ever happened to me."

Chapter 8

Learn from your mistake and never repeat it

Think back to the last mistake that you made at work. Even if it was a little one, like spilling coffee on a paper seconds before you were due to deliver it, you'll have felt a wave of stress and then had the agony of setting things right.

No one is immune to making blunders - we are human, after all! But if we only apologize and continue as before, we're in danger of repeating the same errors.

When we don't learn from our blunders, we put more stress on ourselves and others, and we risk losing people's confidence and trust in us. In this piece, we look at techniques to ensure that we take those lessons on board and then implement what we learn.

Here are five strategies that help you to learn from your mistakes, and to put what you find into practice.

Note: "Making a mistake" is not the same thing as "failing." A failure is the aftermath of a faulty action, whereas a mistake usually itself the erroneous behavior. So, when you make a mistake, you may learn from it and remedy it, but you can only learn from a failure.

1. Own Your Mistakes

You can't learn anything from a mistake until you recognize that you've made one. So, take a huge breath and admit to yours, and then take ownership of it. Notify individuals who need to know, apologize, and inform them that you're working on a solution.

Saying "sorry" needs fortitude, but it's far better to be straight than to hide your error or, worse, to blame others for it. In the long run, people will remember your courage and honesty long after they've forgotten the original misstep.

If, however, they hear about it from another source, your reputation may suffer and you may not obtain another opportunity to learn.

2. Reframe the Error

How you understand your blunders determines the way that you react to them, and what you do next.

Chances are, you'll consider your blunder in a wholly negative perspective for as long as the initial shock and anguish over it endure. But, if you can reframe your blunder as an opportunity to learn, you will motivate yourself to become more knowledgeable and resilient.

When you've acknowledged your mistake, think about what you could do to keep it from happening again. For example, if you didn't follow a method properly, consider establishing a more thorough checklist or a better process manual.

Pause beating yourself up, stop for a minute to contemplate, and start thinking about how you may gain from the scenario.

Tip: Your viewpoint has a major influence on how you understand your blunders and, consequently, on how you react to them.

If you have a "growth" attitude, you likely regard blunders as an opportunity to progress, and not as something that you are bound to repeat because your mindset is "trapped" on the idea that you can't change.
3. Analyze Your Mistake

Next, you need to examine your blunder honestly and objectively. Ask yourself the following questions:

What was I trying to do?
What went wrong?
When did things go wrong?
Why did everything go wrong?

4. Put Lessons Learned Into Practice

The challenge at this time is that employment obligations lure you back to your daily tasks and habitual routines. The lessons that you underlined in Step 3 could languish, unrealized, as merely good intentions. In other words, learning lessons is one thing, but putting them into practice is quite another!

Chances are, acting on what you've learned will involve the discipline and resolve to improve your habits, or to change the way that your team functions. Doing so will enable you to avoid self-sabotage in the future, and will allow you to enjoy the advantages and rewards of using better work habits.

Here, you need to identify the skills, knowledge, resources, or tools that will safeguard you from repeating the error.

Do it with care, though, as "quick fixes" will frequently lead to following difficulties. Any efforts that you take to implement your learning need to be enduring, and something that you can commit to.

If your error was a tiny or a large one, personal goals and action plans will build the framework for implementing the lessons you've learnt. They may supply you with a timeframe to work to, and a list of the duties that you'll need to perform.

The specific instruments that you apply from then on will rely on the unique lessons that you need to put into practice.

For example, if you noticed that a mistake arose owing to your forgetfulness, aides-mémoire or improved attention to detail could help. If you noticed that your organizational talents were below par, digital planners and spreadsheets can be beneficial.

Or, if you realized that a mistake occurred due to a cross-cultural misunderstanding, your communication skills might need a polish.

If the blunder was more organizational than personal, you may need to apply the lesson in a more far-reaching method. Writing clearer methods, for example, could aid to ensure that more gets done without faults.

And, if you determined that your new product wasn't distinctive enough to be successful, you may need to reconsider your whole strategy.

5. Review Your Progress

You may have to try out many techniques to put your lesson into practice before you find one that properly saves you from repeating earlier failures. The Plan-Do-Check-Act cycle is a good strategy for identifying the most effective solutions.

From there, assess the efficiency of your selected strategy by reviewing the amount and kind of mistakes that do – or don't! – still gets produced. Asking someone to keep you accountable may assist you to stay devoted to your new course of action.

Chapter 9

Be happy with the success of others

It's simple to tell when we aren't showing up for folks. To the recipient, it hurts when others cannot step outside of their tale to be happy for you. But on the flip side: It might be tricky to show up with delight and excitement for someone else when you're not in the finest mental condition.

When you're not precisely where you want to be, it might hurt to:

- See others in happy relationships

- Watch folks travel

- Browse social media and witness people having fun

• See your pals doing stuff with someone besides you

The good news: It is possible to applaud people while you're not where you want to be.

Here, are a few suggestions to assist you.

1. Step Outside Yourself

People who compare themselves to others are preoccupied with what they're not doing or how they might be or should be doing something. Stepping outside of yourself makes it simpler to not compare your tale to someone else's.

Challenge yourself to recognize what you are doing or do have. This will remind you that even if you don't have the item you envy in someone else, you have other things you're thankful for.
Tweet

If you find yourself not being able to be glad for others, take efforts to work through your concerns by contemplating the following:

• What's going on in the life that's leading me to feel this way?

• What about this circumstance appears the hardest component to accept?

• What can I do to demonstrate my support for this other person?

Also: Challenge yourself to recognize what you are doing or do have. This will remind you that even if you don't have the item you envy in someone else, you have other things you're thankful for.

2. Name How You're Feeling

While it can be simpler to pretend it doesn't upset you that, for example, your closest buddy recently got engaged, expressing how you feel is crucial.

When your underlying feeling is acknowledged, such as "I feel jealous when____," you may go with the emotion and begin the healing process.

Naming the feeling itself might help defuse it—it enables you to choose how you want to react to your emotions.

Some significant emotions that could be at play:

Is it Jealousy? Perhaps you're jealous. Jealousy is one of the most difficult emotions to confess to experiencing since we conceive of it as an unpleasant sensation.

Jealousy sounds like: "Why aren't you constantly doing something great?" "I wish that was happening for me."

Is it Self-Pity? If you're engaged in self-pity, you could find yourself turning up with fewer energy than normal.

Self-Pity sounds like: "Good for you. Those type of stuff never happened to me." "I wish I could accomplish stuff like that, but I can't."

Is it depression? One of the primary signs of depression is no longer having the energy to accomplish activities you previously liked.

Depression sounds like: "I would want to be able to accomplish that, too, but I don't have the energy." "I used to have the energy to do that. Now, I can hardly remain on top of my everyday tasks."

Are you anxious? When you're nervous, the concept of having objectives and not accomplishing them is unsettling.

Anxiety sounds like: “I would want to attempt something, but I fear...” “I don’t believe I’d be able to achieve it."

3. Identify Areas In Your Life That You Want To Improve

It might be hard to applaud someone else going for their ambitions when your aspirations seem uncertain.

If you’re not sure about your objectives, push yourself to write them down—yes, on actual paper with a pen. For each objective, establish a 3-step action plan so you know how to get started.

Then, assign yourself a fair timeframe. “Reasonable” implies taking into consideration what you have going on in other aspects of your life and what you are personally capable of achieving.

By defining your objectives and concrete action plans to get there, you can cheer others on sincerely.

4. Congratulate Others Even When It's Tough

Even when it's difficult, tell someone, "Congrats." I know, it might seem tough. But there are a few ways to put it: "That sounds excellent, tell me more." "That's amazing." "You've worked hard and it's paying off." "Let's celebrate." "How can I assist you?"

Cheering others on really enhances your connection with other people, and it may help you flip your mental script of viewing their triumph as something to encourage you—not lead you into a comparison spiral.

You would desire the same conduct in return. Practice a few ways to praise people such as "That's terrific, that's incredible, or you're excellent at____."

Cheering others on really enhances your connection with other people, and it may help you perceive their triumph as something to encourage you—not lead you into a comparison spiral.

5. Talk to People About Their Success

If ideas like "How are they smashing it, and why aren't I?" creep up, use it as an entrance point for you to be intrigued and find out.

Are you clear on the road to success? If not, ask your successful buddy about what it took for them to get to where they are. I'm sure along the way they faced some bumps on the road.

Or: Spend some time listening to the non-linear routes other individuals took to accomplish their objectives. Without Fail and Entrepreneur On Fire are two of my favorite podcasts where folks are candid about their mistakes. It helps to hear that people are not always winning and that you may win then fail than win again.

6. Change the Way You Talk To Yourself

The way you speak to yourself could be your greatest challenge. Speak to yourself nicely. The voice in your brain should represent drive and inspiration, not doubt and fear.

Try putting down “I am” phrases, and following it up with something nice. For example: “I am successful in my career.” “I am capable of making progress.”

Also, specify your phrases. For example: If you want to be successful in your profession, evaluate what your concept of success is. Your concept of success may appear different from someone else’s.

7. Address What Holds You Back From Being a Better Version of Yourself

If you're feeling stuck, check into why.

- What people, ideas, and things are holding you back?

- Are you spending too much time with negative people?

- Do you believe in yourself?

- Are you wasting your time exploring social media and looking at other people reaching their goals?

Despite how things look for others, genuine success takes effort—and it needs understanding what you want that work to be and connecting profoundly with why you want to accomplish it.

Despite how things look for others, genuine success takes effort—and it needs understanding what you want that work to be and connecting profoundly with why you want to accomplish it.

Be compassionate to yourself if you slip into the comparison trap, but know you're capable of getting out of it. Even better: You can utilize it to help you develop into the person you want to be on your terms.

Take time to be alone

People tend to be social creatures, and research has shown that social connections are vital for both emotional and physical well-being. However, alone time also plays a pivotal role in mental health. Being around other people comes with rewards, but it also creates stress. You worry about what people think. You alter your behavior to avoid rejection and to fit in with the rest of the group.

While it may be the cost of being part of a social world, some of these challenges demonstrate why alone time can be so important. Having time for yourself gives you the chance to break free from social pressures and tap into your own thoughts, feelings, and experiences.

Chapter 10

Why Alone Time Is Important

Finding time to be alone may offer several major advantages. Some of them include:

- Personal exploration
- Creativity
- Social energy
- Personal Exploration

Becoming comfortable in your own business might allow you the time and flexibility to properly pursue your hobbies without hindrance. It may be a means to try new things, explore subjects that excite you, gain information, and even practice new techniques of self-expression.

Giving yourself alone time means you may examine these topics without the demands and judgments that others may impose. Having time to oneself is crucial for growth and personal development. Instead of worrying about the needs, interests, and views that others may have, alone time allows you to concentrate on yourself.

Creativity

Alone time is a chance to let your thoughts roam and boost your creativity. Without the need to care for or communicate with other people, you may disregard outside influences and concentrate inward.

Research reveals that being alone might lead to changes in the brain that assist fuel the creative process. One research indicated that persons who prefer to purposefully retreat to spend time alone also tend to be highly creative people.

In a 2020 study published in the journal Nature Communications, researchers discovered that perceived social isolation (aka loneliness) is linked to increased activity in the brain networks connected to creativity. When left with a lack of social engagement, the brain cranks up its creative networks to help fill the hole.

Social Energy

Living alone tends to be perceived in a bad way. However, experts have discovered that individuals who live alone may have better social lives and greater social energy than persons who cohabitate with others.

In his book "Going Solo," sociologist Eric Klineberg reports that one in seven U.S. adults lives alone. Klineberg observed that not only were these folks not lonely, but many also had a greater social life.

Signs You Need Some Alone Time

It's not always simple to detect the symptoms that you may need some time apart from other people. Some symptoms to look for include:

- Feeling short-tempered

- Getting easily upset by sometimes simple things
- Losing interest in doing activities with other people
- Feeling overwhelmed or overstimulated
- Having difficulties focusing
- Getting apprehensive about spending time with other people

The good news is that even if you are battling with any of these indications, a little alone time may have a huge therapeutic impact. In one research, persons who reported spending around 11% of their time alone exhibited less unpleasant sentiments in following demanding social situations.

How to Spend Time Alone

If you are thinking about spending some time alone, it is crucial to do so in ways that are healthy for your mental well-being.

Being alone is most good when it is voluntary. It’s also crucial that you feel like you can return to your social environment anytime you choose.

Pick a time: Figure out when you’d want to spend some time alone. Plan that time into your calendar and make sure that other people know that they shouldn’t disrupt you during that time.

Turn off social media: Work on reducing distractions, especially ones that attract social comparisons. Your emphasis should be on your ideas and interests and not on what other people are doing.

Plan something: Not everyone is comfortable spending time alone, so you may find it beneficial to plan out what you want to do. This can entail some relaxing time, enjoying a beloved pastime, or reading a book.

Take a walk: Research has indicated that going outdoors may have a favorable influence on well-being. If you're feeling

cramped up and constrained by too much social engagement, spending a little time outside by yourself enjoying a change of environment might have a healing impact.
There's no precise amount of solitary time that works for everyone. Think of activities that you may want to do by yourself, then start practicing doing them alone.

Creating Space to Be Alone
Finding time to be alone isn't always simple. Those around you may have various social demands and may not appreciate your desire for solitude. Family duties and parental responsibilities might often make it harder to carve out time to oneself. Some things that you can't do to guarantee that you obtain the time you need:

Be clear: Tell the individuals around you, whether they be roommates, family members, or your spouse, that you need time alone.

Be specific: Let folks know about what this implies. For example, you may argue that you require a particular length of undisturbed time to read a book, watch a television program, or listen to a podcast.

Return the favor: If individuals are ready to take measures to guarantee that you receive some alone time, you must offer them the same attention. Offer to take on some chores while they have some space to themselves.

Be flexible: If you are attempting to find time for yourself while you don't live alone or are living in tight quarters with other people, you'll probably need to be flexible and search for chances to carve out time for yourself.

Try getting up early in the morning to spend some calm time to yourself before others in the home start to wake. If that isn't a possibility, doing things like going for a walk outside or having other family members babysit the kids or taking over domestic responsibilities while you take a break might be useful.

Develop the Right Mindset

If the prospect of being alone makes you dread that you'll wind up feeling lonely, research says it may be good to reframe time spent alone as solitude. In one research, participants were allocated to either read about the prevalence of loneliness, read a text extolling the advantages of isolation, or read about an irrelevant issue. 13

After finishing this reading, the participants sat alone for a 10-minute interval. In each scenario, respondents reported reductions in both unpleasant and good sensations. Such findings imply that although being alone may not always increase your mood, it might help you better manage your emotions.

The research also indicated that although persons who read about the advantages of isolation didn't always have a higher mood, they didn't have the same drop of good sentiments that those in the other two groups experienced.

Chapter 11

Results take time

Mental toughness is like a muscle. It has to be worked on to grow and develop. If you haven't pushed yourself in hundreds of minor ways, of course, you'll wilt when things become truly challenging.

But it doesn't have to be that way.

Choose to complete the tenth rep when it would be easy to simply do nine. Choose to produce when it would be easy to consume. Choose to ask the additional inquiry when it would be easy to accept. Prove to yourself — in a thousand subtle ways — that you have the courage to step in the ring and do fight with life.

Mental toughness is acquired via modest victories. It's the individual decisions that we make on a daily basis that create our "mental toughness muscle." We all desire mental strength, but you can't think your way to it. It's your bodily deeds that indicate your mental fortitude.

Mental toughness isn't about gaining a tremendous dose of inspiration or bravery. It's about creating everyday routines that enable you to keep to a plan and overcome problems and distractions again and over and over again.

Mentally strong individuals don't have to be bolder, more skilled, or more bright – simply more consistent. Mentally tough individuals build methods that help them concentrate on the essential things regardless of how many barriers life throws in front of them. It's their behaviors that build the basis of their mental ideas and eventually set them apart.

I've written about this many times before. Here are the fundamental stages for creating a new habit and links to extra information on accomplishing each step.

Start by developing your identity.
Focus on little actions, not life-changing changes.
Develop a habit that gets you moving regardless of how motivated you feel.
Stick to the timetable and forget about the outcomes.
When you fall up, get back on track as fast as possible.
Mental toughness boils down to your habits. It's about doing the things you know you're meant to do on a more regular basis. It's

about your devotion to regular practice and your ability to keep to a routine.

Achievers and high performers from all walks of life endure ups and downs along the way to success—they battle failure, burnout, discouragement, exhaustion, self-limiting beliefs, stress, and so much more.

How do some individuals consistently work towards their objectives year after year while others give up on them? How can those folks remain strong and endure when there is so much stacked against them?

Studies now demonstrate that mental power is a significant factor in success. People with strong levels of mental toughness may push past these difficulties and establish a route towards achievement, whereas others with weaker levels of mental toughness may quit their aspirations.

The good news is that no matter who you are, what you've been taught, or what you presently think, you can build the mental toughness you need to be successful.

Chapter 12

Maintaining mental health

7 techniques to increase mental strength and build resilience

There are various parallels between physical exercise and mental health - not the least of which is the significance of your daily practices. These regular activities will pay off on important occasions when your mental toughness is required, too.

Developing mental power entails adopting activities in each of these 7 areas:

1. Mindfulness

When you exercise mindfulness, you strengthen your capacity to respond instead of reacting. It allows you to slow down the stimulus-reaction cycle so you may select a response that works for you. Over time, this talent will come in helpful when you least anticipate it – but most need it. You could find yourself less apprehensive while talking to your boss, or less prone to create disputes with your spouse.

There are various sorts of mindfulness practices, so select whatever one you love and matches your lifestyle. Try focused breathing, strolling meditation, or taking a virtual yoga session.

2. Work with a professional

Working with a mental health expert or coach may be incredibly useful in gaining mental strength. After all, the combat you're most typically waging occurs in your thoughts. Coaches and therapists are both incredibly good at helping you to fight negative thinking patterns so that they don't mindlessly rule your behavior.

Psychotherapists commonly achieve this by employing CBT, or cognitive behavioral therapy. This approach is very effective for mental health conditions including sadness and anxiety. Coaches, on the other hand, may assist you with accountability as you work towards your objectives. They may assist reframe disappointments, preventing you from relapsing into negative habits, and keeping you motivated.

3. Keep a notebook

If you want to check in with your mental strength regularly, maintaining a diary is a terrific option. It may help you maintain tabs on your improvement throughout time, which is wonderful for increasing your self-esteem.

There are no restrictions on what you post in your journal. Try free-writing for several minutes, goal-setting, or making notes of any pressures that feel especially overwhelming. Sometimes, the act of putting things down helps our minds begin to work through our issues. It's a little step away from being overwhelmed and towards feeling in control.

4. Practice self-compassion

Many of us assume that we'll somehow be more productive if we beat ourselves up, but that's not the case. Building self-compassion truly helps us create resilience. Focusing on what we do well — instead of all of our shortcomings — puts us in a development mentality while avoiding the negative cycle. It lets us say, "That didn't go so well, but here's what I learned — and how I can do better next time."

5. Get out of your comfort zone

Want to discover whether you've learned the key abilities of mental toughness? Throw yourself in the deep end! Like many talents, mental strength can't be acquired without practice. At some time, you may have to do something new, unknown, or dangerous – and that's a good thing.

Start small or start large - it doesn't matter. Sign up for a class, get coffee with someone who intimidates you, or applies for your ideal job on LinkedIn. Whatever it is, pay attention to how you react when fearful sensations come up. Write them down in your diary, and then answer them as you would to a close friend. You'll find that you are capable of undertaking hard things – and you may even love them.

6. Develop a routine

If you were growing physical strength, you'd perform repetitions at the gym. To increase mental strength, you have to establish regular routines that reinforce the new abilities that you're exercising.

Journaling, practicing mindfulness, and connecting with a coach may all be part of this regimen. You want to prioritize everything that inspires you to pause, reflect, and question. Choose ideas and activities that help you feel secure.

Be sure that your daily routine also incorporates self-care techniques. Often, when individuals are on the "personal development bandwagon," they believe that every element of their lives has to be "optimized." Start small and build up. Prioritize fundamental well-being, such as getting adequate rest, checking for the indicators of physical and mental weariness, and being attentive about what you eat.

7. Keep your ties strong

One of the biggest determinants of life pleasure is our interactions with others. Don't attempt to do it all alone. We need to have loved ones near to us – to celebrate our triumphs, encourage us onward, and console us in terrible times.

Your support system is your therapist and your coach, but it's also your friends and family. Don't forget to enjoy yourself. Have fun, spend time with the people you love, and do things that make you happy. Joy insulates us against stress and keeps us going when we want to give up the battle.

Mental strength isn't only about pushing ahead, just as physical strength isn't about working out all the time. It's about understanding how to achieve balance – to both work and play, to love and lose, to push and praise, with equal ease and grace.

www.ingramcontent.com/pod-product-compliance
Lightning Source LLC
LaVergne TN
LVHW050318160826
845677LV00014B/3456